70 Millennial Problems with Wisdom Solutions
Richard W. Linford

I am an attorney at law, and have served as an advertising and marketing executive, a copy and slogan and technical writer, as CEO, Executive VP and VP broadcast and other business executive in several companies, one of which was one of the largest privately owned broadcasting companies. I am an oil and acrylic and watercolor artist, my art is found on fineartamerica.com. I have written multiple non-fiction and fiction books which are found on amazon.com. I served as state chairman of the National Conference of Christians and Jews (and Muslims) and as chairman of a multi-county Red Cross. I currently serve on the state Volunteers Active in Disaster (VOAD) board. I am an active member of The Church of Jesus Christ of Latter-day Saints. I am married to the most remarkable woman in the world and am dad to 8 children and granddad to 27 grandchildren.

Foreword. I have chosen to write about 70 Millennial Problems with Wisdom Solutions because we are smart people and we are capable of solving these problems and ushering in a millennial era of peace and prosperity for all, and not just for Americans. This small book is thought to be of value to elected politicians, legislators, city, county, state, federal government employees, attorneys, accountants, students of political science, and any person who thinks about a better world for all. You may differ regarding solutions. You may also think solutions stated are simplistic. Not to worry. This writing, imperfect and short though it admitted, is a thought piece set forth to help us focus and think.

1. Abortion
    1.1. Problem. 300,000,000+ unborn babies have been surgically and chemically murdered, killed, flushed, hacked apart, sold for body parts, dissolved, sent to landfills since Roe v Wade: genocide 50,000,000+ BLACKS, genocide 50,000,000+ HISPANICS, genocide 200,000,000+ Jewish American, Native American, Asian American, Caucasian babies.
    1.2. Solutions. Adoption. Defund Planned Parenthood and all abortion providers. Elect and appoint anti-abortion advocates. Overturn Roe v Wade and like case law and legislation. Anti-abortion legislation.
    1.3. NOTES:

2. Agriculture
   2.1. Problem. Drought. Fires. Production shortfalls. Effect of tariffs.
   2.2. Solutions. Farm, Ranch subsidies. Research funding. Eliminate tariffs on Ag products.
   2.3. NOTES:

3. Alcohol
    3.1. Problem. Alcoholism.
    3.2. Solutions. Don't drink alcohol at all. If you drink, drink responsibly. Get 12 steps or other
        help if alcoholic.
    3.3. NOTES:

4. Artificial Intelligence and Robotics
   4.1. Problems. AI and Robotic threat to humans.
   4.2. Solutions. Code of ethics. Monitoring. Legislation.
   4.3. NOTES:

5. Capitalism
    5.1. Problem. Inordinate amount of wealth held by a very few persons.
    5.2. Solutions. Greater taxation of the extremely wealthy. Pledge to deploy wealth to solve world's serious problems such as hunger and disease.
    5.3. NOTES:

6. Children
    6.1. Problem. Abuse
    6.2. Solutions. Child abuse hotline. Stiff penalties.
    6.3. NOTES:

7. China
    7.1. Problems. Trade imbalance. Military build-up.
    7.2. Solutions. Military parity. Meetings President Xi Jinping and POTUS. Sanctions.
    7.3. NOTES:

8. Civil Rights
    8.1. Problems. Violations. Hate crimes.
    8.2. Solutions. Stiff penalties.
    8.3. NOTES:

9. Communism
    9.1. Problems. Serious threat to freedoms.
    9.2. Solutions. Monitor. Stiff penalties.
    9.3. NOTES:

10. Conflict Afghanistan
    10.1.   Problem. Volatility.
    10.2.   Solutions. Peace keeping force.
    10.3.   NOTES:

11. Conflict Africa
    11.1.   Problem. Stealing land.
    11.2.   Solutions. Sanctions.
    11.3.   NOTES:

12. Conflict Arab Israeli

    12.1.   Problem. Conflict.

    12.2.   Solutions. Two state solution? One state solution? Jerusalem is capital.

    12.3.   NOTES:

13. Conflict Iran
   13.1.   Problem. Volatility.
   13.2.   Solutions. Sanctions.
   13.3.   NOTES:

14. Conflict Iraq
    14.1.   Problem. Volatility.
    14.2.   Solutions. Peace keeping force.
    14.3.   NOTES:

15. Conflict North Korea

    15.1.   Problem. Threat to U.S.; Oppressing NK people.

    15.2.   Solutions. Meetings with Kim Jong Un; Denuclearize Korean Peninsula.

    15.3.   NOTES:

16. Conflict Russia
    16.1.   Problem. Russian military build-up.
    16.2.   Solutions. Military parity. Meetings with Russian President and POTUS.
        Strengthen NATO.
    16.3.   NOTES:

17. Conflict Syria.
    17.1.   Problem. Volatility.
    17.2.   Solutions. Sanctions. Military force.
    17.3.   NOTES:

18. Climate Change and Environment
    18.1.   Problem. Man's activities affect the environment.
    18.2.   Solutions. Monitoring. Whistle blower. Stiff penalties for pollution.
    18.3.   NOTES:

19. Crime

    19.1.   Problem. Murder, Rape, Burglary, Theft.

    19.2.   Solutions. Speedy death penalty for murder, rape, and burglary with weapon. Allow stop and frisk. Stop and search. Allow and legally protect community citizen police.

    19.3.   NOTES:

20. Crime - Prisons

20.1.	Problem. Inordinate number in prisons. Immense expense. Overcrowding.

20.2.	Solutions. Release all drug use offenders. Release all non-Americans to their own countries. Create categories. Release all minimum offenders. Eliminate all private prisons.

20.3.	NOTES:

21. Crime – White Collar

    21.1.   Problem. Fraud, Embezzlement.

    21.2.   Solutions. Stiff penalties. Forfeiture.

    21.3.   NOTES:

22. Disease
    22.1.   Problem. Epidemics.
    22.2.   Solutions. Monitor. Research funds. Emergency preparedness.
    22.3.   NOTES:

23. Drug abuse

    23.1.   Problem. Heroin; Meth; Opioids; Marijuana.

    23.2.   Solutions. Military, Border Patrol, ICE shut down traffic. Stiffer penalties, Medical Marijuana allowed. Chemical reversal of addiction. Militarily destroy source of drugs.

    23.3.   NOTES:

24. Education access
   24.1.   Problem. Many prevented from higher education due to entry requirements.
   24.2.   Solutions. Eliminate GRE. Allow all to enter online Open University.
   24.3.   NOTES:

25. Education expense

    25.1.   Problem. Expense of higher education resulting in crushing student debt.

    25.2.   Solutions. Forgive all student debt.

    25.3.   NOTES:

26. Education safety

    26.1.   Problem. Vulnerability of schools and teachers and professors.

    26.2.   Solutions. Arm all teachers and professors who will. Arm and protect all schools.

    26.3.   NOTES:

27. Emergency Preparedness

    27.1.   Problem. Accident, Conflict, Economy, Terrorist, War, Weather – related negative events.

    27.2.   Solutions. Advance response: arms, communications, energy/heat, equipment, food, medical, medicine, money, sanitation, security, shelter, recovery, tools, and water.

    27.3.   NOTES:

28. Energy
    28.1.   Problem. Reliance on Arab and other energy sources coupled with attendant loss
        of treasure.
    28.2.   Solutions. Energy independence – drilling, solar, wind, etc.
    28.3.   NOTES:

29. Existential

    29.1.   Problem. Despair. Fear. Depression.

    29.2.   Solutions. Christians follow Christ. Prepare for Second Coming.

    29.3.   NOTES:

30. Family

    30.1.   Problem. Disintegration. Divorce.

    30.2.   Solutions. Marriage as between a man and woman. Domestic abuse hotline.

    30.3.   NOTES:

31. Food

    31.1.   Problem. Shortage. Distribution. Hunger.

    31.2.   Solutions. Research. Ag assistance. No person hungry program. Fast one day per month. Give equivalent value of meals missed to food banks.

    31.3.   NOTES:

32. Freedom

  32.1.   Problem. Tendency of all in power to curtail freedom of those not in power.

  32.2.   Solutions. Constitution.

  32.3.   NOTES:

33. Freedom of Religion

    33.1.   Problem. Disbelievers and believers compelling others to believe as they believe.

    33.2.   Solutions. Respect and allow all men, women, children to worship how, where, or what they may so long as they do not coerce others to believe and worship as they do.

    33.3.   NOTES:

34. Freedom of Speech

    34.1.   Problem. One group compelling another group to refrain from speaking.

    34.2.   Solutions. Respect and allow all men, women, children to speak how, where, or what they may so long as they do not incite to riot.

    34.3.   NOTES:

35. Freedom to bear arms
    35.1.   Problem. Government controls arms. Select groups control arms.
    35.2.   Solutions. Allow all to arm themselves according to certain constraints.
    35.3.   NOTES:

36. Globalism

    36.1.   Problem. Advocacy of end of nations, end of borders.

    36.2.   Solutions. Nationalism. Sealed borders. All enter by the front door and are vetted and E-verified.

    36.3.   NOTES:

37. Health

    37.1.   Problem. Insurance. Disease.

    37.2.   Solution. Mandated low cost health insurance. Competition cross state lines.
        Added research funds.

    37.3.   NOTES:

38. Human trafficking
    38.1.   Problem. Coyotes moving women, children, and men, controlling their lives,
        imposing prostitution.
    38.2.   Solutions. Severe penalties for human trafficking. Human trafficking hotlines.
    38.3.   NOTES:

39. Immigration
    39.1.   Problem. Unenforced immigration laws. Porous borders. Sanctuary cities and
        other political entities.
    39.2.   Solutions. Increase ICE. Increase border patrol. Secure the borders. Kate's law.
    39.3.   NOTES:

40. Incivility and Politically Correct rules

    40.1.   Problem. Verbal abuse. Hate crimes. Onerous politically correct rules.

    40.2.   Solutions. Respect. Aggressive prosecution of any hate crime. Eliminate politically correct rules.

    40.3.   NOTES:

41. Infrastructure
    41.1.   Problem. Deteriorating airports, ports, roads, electrical grids, sewage systems, water systems.
    41.2.   Solutions. Fund major infrastructure renewal projects. Divert Middle East and other war money to infrastructure.
    41.3.   NOTES:

42. Jobs
    42.1.   Problem. Jobs taken by foreign nationals.
    42.2.   Solutions. Hire American Citizens. Hire American Citizens first.
    42.3.   NOTES:

43. Latchkey Children

    43.1.   Problem. Several millions of children raised in one parent homes.

    43.2.   Solutions. Latchkey children hotlines. Funding for single parents to be home for children.

    43.3.   NOTES:

44. Manufacturing

44.1.	Problem. Ceded and ceding control of manufacturing to foreign nations.

44.2.	Solutions. Incenting U.S. manufacturing.

44.3.	NOTES:

45. Marriage

    45.1.   Problem. Dissolution. Divorces. Broken homes. Mischaracterization.

    45.2.   Solutions. Love at home. Make divorce much more difficult. Between man and woman.

    45.3.   NOTES:

46. Medicine
    46.1.   Problem. Shortage. Expense.
    46.2.   Solutions. Stockpile. Set limits on medicine expense.
    46.3.   NOTES:

47. Military Readiness
    47.1.   Problem. Lack of funding. Lack of competence. Lack of armament.
    47.2.   Solutions. Fund a ready, fully capable, alert military.
    47.3.   NOTES:

48. Morals and Ethics
    48.1.   Problem. Relativism. Corruption
    48.2.   Solutions. Jesus Christ principles.
    48.3.   NOTES:

49. Economy

    49.1.   Problem. Focus on GDP.

    49.2.   Solutions. Focus on National production output.

    49.3.   NOTES:

50. Natural Resources
    50.1.   Problem. Pollution. Environment negative impact.
    50.2.   Solutions. Fines. Jail time. Encourage whistle blowing.
    50.3.   NOTES:

51. Nuclear Threat
   51.1.   Problem. Thousands of Nuclear weapons unevenly distributed. Dirty bomb in
   populated area.
   51.2.   Solutions. Negotiate reduction in number. Negotiate their elimination altogether.
   51.3.   NOTES:

52. Political Abuse
    52.1.   Problem. Government abuse of citizens.
    52.2.   Solutions. Whistle blower statute. Auditor general.
    52.3.   NOTES:

53. Political Corruption

    53.1.   Problem. Politicians and appointed government officers profiting pay to play during and security clearance access after their term.

    53.2.   Solution. Set legal limits. Require disgorgement and fines. Require serious jail time.

    53.3.   NOTES:

54. Population
    54.1.   Problem. Replacement lags.
    54.2.   Solutions. Tax incentives for children and families.
    54.3.   NOTES:

55. Prosperity
  55.1.   Problem. Curtailed because of military spending abroad and lower cost
    production abroad and ability to harbor funds offshore.
  55.2.   Solutions. Bring back military and manufacturing and offshore $ from abroad.
  55.3.   NOTES:

56. Prostitution
    56.1.   Problem. More women engaged in. Robots.
    56.2.   Solutions. Stiff laws against.
    56.3.   NOTES:

57. Racism

    57.1.   Problem. Conflict between races.

    57.2.   Solutions. Respect. Clamp down on hate crimes. Clamp down on media fomenting racial discord.

    57.3.   NOTES:

58. Resources

    58.1.   Problem. Scarce.

    58.2.   Solutions. Explore and prove out new sources. Stockpile.

    58.3.   NOTES:

59. Rights of Men

    59.1.   Problem. Men denigrated. Purveyors of philosophy of "toxic masculinity."

    59.2.   Solutions. Honor men for their significant roles which differ from roles of women.

    59.3.   NOTES:

60. Rights of Races

    60.1.   Problem. Racial divides.

    60.2.   Solutions. Respect. Civil rights for all.

    60.3.   NOTES:

61. Rights of Women

    61.1.   Problem. Women or Men treated as second class citizens.

    61.2.   Solutions. Eliminate glass ceilings. Eliminate discrimination.

    61.3.   NOTES:

62. Safety.
    62.1.   Problem. Porous borders. Illegal aliens. Gangs.
    62.2.   Solutions. Close the borders. Vet and everify illegal immigrants. Roundup and
        deport gang members.
    62.3.   NOTES:

63. Sex and Violence in Media
  63.1.   Problem. Sex and violence contrary to morals.
  63.2.   Solutions. Allow safe filters. Shut down all child pornography. Shut down
     pornography in general
  63.3.   NOTES:

64. Socialism

    64.1.   Problem. Contrary to constitutional democracy.

    64.2.   Solutions. Up-hold constitution.

    64.3.   NOTES:

65. Space Exploration

    65.1.   Problem. Exploring the moon, mars, and beyond.

    65.2.   Solutions. Provide funding. Establish a Space Force.

    65.3.   NOTES:

66. Taxation

    66.1.   Problem. High taxes.

    66.2.   Solutions. Lower taxes especially for middle class.

    66.3.   NOTES:

67. Terrorism
    67.1.   Problem. Terrorists.
    67.2.   Solutions. E-verify; Seal borders except at designated points. See something say something.
    67.3.   NOTES:

68. Tobacco

    68.1.   Problem. Cancer.

    68.2.   Solutions. Continue warnings. Allow significant legal verdicts against tobacco companies.

    68.3.   NOTES:

69. Water

    69.1.   Problem. Shortage of safe water.

    69.2.   Solutions. Water from air technology. Water from grapheme filters technology. Water from solar energy driven distillation.

    69.3.   NOTES:

70. Whistle Blower

    70.1.   Problem. Whistle blowers prevented from blowing the whistle. Targeted after the fact by those referenced.

    70.2.   Solutions. Stringently enforce laws protecting whistle blowers. Easier system allowing blowing whistle on corruption and misdeeds of government or corporate officers or entities.

    70.3.   NOTES:

71. OTHER

    71.1.   PROBLEMS?

    71.2.   SOLUTIONS?

    71.3.   NOTES:

Writings – Books and eBooks Catalog. Richard W. Linford. August 2018

My book subjects and titles, most of which are found at
 www. amazon.com. Click on the provided link or Type Richard W. Linford or Richard Linford.

1. <u>ABS OF STEEL.</u> HOW TO BUILD SIX-PACK ABS OF STEEL THE QUALITY REP WAY! Man or Woman! In the Privacy of your own home! https://www.amazon.com/HOW-BUILD-SIX-PACK-STEEL-QUALITY-ebook/dp/B010EM6MY6/ref=sr_1_85?ie=UTF8&qid=1502472532&sr=8-85&keywords=Richard+W.+Linford

2. <u>ADVERTISING. MARKETING.</u> Jackalope Mindset: Focus on your Jackalope! Break through the social and media clutter. Sell yourself, your products and your services.
3. https://www.amazon.com/Jackalope-Mindset-clutter-yourself-services-ebook/dp/B01LG786EW/ref=sr_1_35?ie=UTF8&qid=1502472693&sr=8-35&keywords=Richard+W.+Linford

4. ANXIETY. Marty and The UK Brexit High Anxiety Hotel and Restaurant. A short story. An allegory.
5. https://www.amazon.com/Marty-Mouse-Brexit-Anxiety-Restaurant/dp/152109649X/ref=sr_1_49?ie=UTF8&qid=1534870920&sr=8-49&keywords=rICHARD+w+lINFORD

6. BAKING SODA USES? 325 ARM & HAMMER BAKING SODA USES??? (Socium Bicarbonate; Bi-carbonate Soda) USES THAT PEOPLE CLAIM WORK???
7. https://www.amazon.com/325-HAMMER-BAKING-SODA-USES-ebook/dp/B011CF6U0K/ref=sr_1_6?ie=UTF8&qid=1502486878&sr=8-6&keywords=Richard+W+Linford

8. <u>BEST PRACTICE AND BEST PRACTICES.</u> THE POWER OF BEST PRACTICE AND BEST PRACTICES.
9. https://www.amazon.com/Power-Best-Practice-Practices/dp/1521361398/ref=sr_1_24?ie=UTF8&qid=1502473575&sr=8-24&keywords=Richard+W+Linford

10. <u>BLINDING FLASH OF THE OBVIOUS.</u> IN SEARCH OF 500 NOT SO BLINDING AND BLINDING FLASHES OF THE OBVIOUS
11. https://www.amazon.com/SEARCH-500-BLINDING-FLASHES-OBVIOUS-ebook/dp/B01N0EHXVM/ref=sr_1_9?ie=UTF8&qid=1505837336&sr=8-9&keywords=Richard+W.+Linford

12. <u>BRAIN POWER.</u> Better Brain! Super Brain! Supercharge Your Brain! Supercharge Your Brain 1209 Ways!
13. <u>https://www.amazon.com/Better-Brain-Super-Supercharge-Your-ebook/dp/B014EVX8WW/ref=sr_1_14?ie=UTF8&qid=1534865760&sr=8-14&keywords=rICHARD+w+lINFORD</u>

14. <u>BUSINESS TURNAROUND.</u> HOW TO BEGIN TURNING YOUR BUSINESS AROUND IN 30 MINUTES: Save a fortune on consulting services!
15. <u>https://www.amazon.com/BEGIN-TURNING-BUSINESS-AROUND-MINUTES-ebook/dp/B011T55SUG/ref=sr_1_8?ie=UTF8&qid=1505837336&sr=8-8&keywords=Richard+W.+Linford</u>

16. <u>BUSINESS TURNAROUND.</u> Stop Strolling Around Naked In Your Business Empire Like "ALITTLEKINGLY". Begin to turn your business around now.

17. https://www.amazon.com/Strolling-Around-Business-Empire-ALittle/dp/1575740206/ref=sr_1_36?ie=UTF8&qid=1505839392&sr=8-36&keywords=Richard+W.+Linford

18. BUY or LEASE, and DRIVE a FORD AMERICAN "LUXURY" CAR and TRUCK TODAY! 222 AFFIRMATIONS. HONORING FORD MOTOR COMPANY. GREATEST CAR AND TRUCK COMPANY AND BRAND IN THE WORLD. Don't procrastinate. Do it now!

19. https://www.amazon.com/LEASE-DRIVE-AMERICAN-LUXURY-TRUCK-ebook/dp/B07GQBJYP2/ref=sr_1_1?ie=UTF8&qid=1535389923&sr=8-1&keywords=bUY+LEASE+DRIVE+A+FORD&dpID=514BieDNMkL&preST=_SY445_QL70_&dpSrc=srch

20. <u>CONCORD, CALIFORNIA.</u> concord in the Son: honoring concord california.
21. https://www.amazon.com/concord-Son-honoring-california-ebook/dp/B00ZSRASYS/ref=sr_1_34?ie=UTF8&qid=1534868802&sr=8-34&keywords=rICHARD+w+lINFORD

22. <u>DISINTERMEDIATION. INTERMEDIATION.</u> Disintermediation, Intermediation, or Both: 200 steps to greater prosperity by eliminating or adding intermediaries.
23. https://www.amazon.com/Disintermediation-Intermediation-Both-eliminating-intermediaries-ebook/dp/B01DMIJ0DY/ref=sr_1_27?ie=UTF8&qid=1505838733&sr=8-27&keywords=Richard+W.+Linford

24. <u>EMERGENCY PREPAREDNESS.</u> Sleep While The Wind Blows! Survival Checklists! Prepare Now! When a disaster or emergency happens, your time for preparation is over! https://www.amazon.com/Sleep-While-Wind-Blows-preparation-ebook/dp/B00P00RUOO/ref=sr_1_1?ie=UTF8&qid=1534865760&sr=8-1&keywords=rICHARD+w+lINFORD&dpID=51-6x1719WL&preST=_SY445_QL70_&dpSrc=srch

25. <u>FICTION.</u> Andrew Chipman's Christmas Angel.
26. https://www.amazon.com/Andrew-Chipmans-Christmas-Richard-LInford/dp/1575740176/ref=sr_1_38?ie=UTF8&qid=1505839508&sr=8-38&keywords=Richard+W.+Linford

27.   <u>FICTION</u>. Andy Pepper and Prince Kalid's Solid Gold Western Flyer X-53.

28.   https://www.amazon.com/Pepper-Prince-Kahlids-Solid-Western-ebook/dp/B01EYXVZOI/ref=sr_1_76?ie=UTF8&qid=1534878985&sr=8-76&keywords=rICHARD+w+lINFORD

29.   <u>FICTION</u>. Driving Mabel for Christmas Dinner.

30.   https://www.amazon.com/Driving-Christmas-Dinner-Richard-Linford-ebook/dp/B078HB4XC3/ref=sr_1_22?ie=UTF8&qid=1534868802&sr=8-22&keywords=rICHARD+w+lINFORD&dpID=5178sLG1twL&preST=_SY445_QL70_&dpSrc=srch

31. <u>FICTION</u>. I Am the Count of Monte Cristo. Short story.

32.

https://www.amazon.com/s/ref=sr_pg_6?rh=i%3Aaps%2Ck%3ArICHARD+w+lINFORD&page=6&keywords=rICHARD+w+lINFORD&ie=UTF8&qid=1534878985

33. <u>FICTION</u>. JOSHUA REDSHIELD'S DNA AND THE ILLUMINATI? A TECHNOTHRILLER (JOSHUA REDSHIELD AND THE ILLUMINATI Book 1)

34. https://www.amazon.com/JOSHUA-REDSHIELDS-DNA-ILLUMINATI-TECHNOTHRILLER-ebook/dp/B01E91I4S0/ref=sr_1_30?ie=UTF8&qid=1534868802&sr=8-30&keywords=rICHARD+w+lINFORD

35. <u>FICTION</u>. The Bulletproof Invincible Man. Sheik Harun al-Rashid – A short story.

36. https://www.amazon.com/Bulletproof-Invincible-Man-Sheik-al-Rashid-ebook/dp/B011FKPMP6/ref=sr_1_62?ie=UTF8&qid=1534870960&sr=8-62&keywords=rICHARD+w+lINFORD

37. FICTION. The KITE MAKER'S DAUGHTER: A fabled story for every daughter and every son? An allegory.

38. https://www.amazon.com/KITE-MAKERS-DAUGHTER-daughter-allegory/dp/1718028172/ref=sr_1_1?ie=UTF8&qid=1534887731&sr=8-1&keywords=The+KITE+MAKER%27S+Daughter

39. <u>FICTION</u>. The Minimalist: 89 EMAILS TO MY MARINE SON RAFAEL.

40. https://www.amazon.com/Minimalist-EMAILS-MARINE-RAFAEL-novel/dp/1980353794/ref=sr_1_61?ie=UTF8&qid=1534870960&sr=8-61&keywords=rICHARD+w+lINFORD

41. <u>FICTION</u>. The Receiver. A short story about an appointed Securities and Exchange Commission Receiver, his work and response.

42. https://www.amazon.com/Receiver-short-Richard-W-Linford-ebook/dp/B0134GYM2I/ref=sr_1_18?ie=UTF8&qid=1534865760&sr=8-18&keywords=rICHARD+w+lINFORD

43. <u>FICTION</u>. THE WHITE UNICORN CODE: Mystery of the Lady with the Unicorn and other Unicorn tapestries.
44. https://www.amazon.com/White-Unicorn-Code-tapestries-2010-07-21/dp/B01F9GTEM4/ref=sr_1_94?ie=UTF8&qid=1534883070&sr=8-94&keywords=rICHARD+w+lINFORD

45. <u>FICTION.</u> The Young Marine and the Snow an allegory.
46. https://www.amazon.com/Young-Marine-Snow-Allegory/dp/1575740192/ref=sr_1_37?ie=UTF8&qid=1505839508&sr=8-37&keywords=Richard+W.+Linford
47. https://www.amazon.com/Young-Marine-Snow-short-allegory-ebook/dp/B011PHGFH8/ref=sr_1_83?ie=UTF8&qid=1534882887&sr=8-83&keywords=rICHARD+w+lINFORD

48. <u>FICTION.</u> Waiting with Brutus Caesar Anthony the 7th, William and Mary, for SAM THE MECHANIC MAN.

49. https://www.amazon.com/Waiting-Brutus-Anthony-William-MECHANIC/dp/1521158010/ref=sr_1_32?ie=UTF8&qid=1505839176&sr=8-32&keywords=Richard+W.+Linford

50. **<u>FICTION. WESTERN</u>. The Cowboy Bar L Dude Ranch, Five Guests, and the Mean Banker.**

51. https://www.amazon.com/Cowboy-Dude-Ranch-Guests-Banker-ebook/dp/B0756JG4K2/ref=sr_1_27?ie=UTF8&qid=1534868802&sr=8-27&keywords=rICHARD+w+lINFORD

52. <u>HABITS</u>. Seven DEADLY NEGATIVE HABITS of Highly Ineffective People plus The YHoung Knight with the short lance and the Black Knight – An Allegory.
53. https://www.amazon.com/DEADLY-NEGATIVE-HABITS-Highly-Ineffective/dp/1549957171/ref=sr_1_55?ie=UTF8&qid=1534870960&sr=8-55&keywords=rICHARD+w+lINFORD

54. <u>HABITS OF LOSERS.</u> How to Lose! 70 habits of losers who abuse or lose friends, health, influence and money!
55. https://www.amazon.com/How-Lose-habits-friends-influence-ebook/dp/B01AAV6CGO/ref=sr_1_40?ie=UTF8&qid=1534869921&sr=8-40&keywords=rICHARD+w+lINFORD

56. <u>HEALTH.</u> HIGH FRUCTOSE CORN SYRUP AND SUGAR BELLY.

57. https://www.amazon.com/HIGH-FRUCTOSE-SYRUP-SUGAR-BELLY-ebook/dp/B01B554JAK/ref=sr_1_28?ie=UTF8&qid=1505838733&sr=8-28&keywords=Richard+W.+Linford

58. <u>JESUS CHRIST PAPERS</u>. A letter to my grandson, Jason: You are a son of Heavenly Father and Heavenly Mother. I love you. Your grandpa.

59. https://www.amazon.com/letter-grandson-Jason-Heavenly-grandpa-ebook/dp/B01AOWGOQC/ref=sr_1_33?ie=UTF8&qid=1534868802&sr=8-33&keywords=rICHARD+w+lINFORD

60. <u>JESUS CHRIST PAPERS. ANGELS</u>. ARE SHOULDER ANGELS AMONG US? Yes. There are good and bad angels.
61. <u>https://www.amazon.com/ARE-SHOULDER-ANGELS-AMONG-US-ebook/dp/B00Q3GX8Q8/ref=sr_1_12?ie=UTF8&qid=1502487183&sr=8-12&keywords=Richard+W+Linford</u>

62. <u>JESUS CHRIST PAPERS. ARTICLES OF FAITH.</u> My 32 Articles of Faith in God the Father and His Son Jesus Christ: Based on Joseph Smith's 13 Articles of Faith, LDS Gospel Principles, and my understanding of the doctrine and Church of Jesus Christ.
63. <u>https://www.amazon.com/Articles-Faith-Father-Jesus-Christ-ebook/dp/B011DTKQSC/ref=sr_1_10?ie=UTF8&qid=1502487183&sr=8-10&keywords=Richard+W+Linford</u>

64. <u>JESUS CHRIST PAPERS.</u> BEHOLD THE MAN: Jesus is The Christ, The Great Jehovah, The Holy Messiah who soon will come!

65. <u>https://www.amazon.com/Behold-Man-Christ-Jehovah-Messiah-ebook/dp/B011YLLSKO/ref=sr_1_43?ie=UTF8&qid=1534869921&sr=8-43&keywords=rICHARD+w+lINFORD</u>

66. <u>JESUS CHRIST PAPERS</u>. Christmas and Easter Opus. Honoring and testifying that GOD OUR HEAVENLY FATHER AND HIS BELOVED SON LIVE

67. <u>https://www.amazon.com/Christmas-Easter-Opus-Honoring-testifying-ebook/dp/B00ZS53A0O/ref=sr_1_51?ie=UTF8&qid=1534870960&sr=8-51&keywords=rICHARD+w+lINFORD&dpID=51eBFOrba7L&preST=_SY445_QL70_&dpSrc=srch</u>

68. <u>JESUS CHRIST PAPERS.</u> COME KNEEL AT THE FEET OF GOD THE FATHER AND HIS SON JESUS CHRIST AND RECEIVE ETERNAL LIFE

69. <u>JESUS CHRIST PAPERS.</u> COME UNTO CHRIST: REPENT AND PRAY MIGHTILY FOR FORGIVENESS OF YOUR SINS! Meditations on Repentance, Prayer, and The Book of Mormon, Book of Enos: The Jesus Christ papers

70. https://www.amazon.com/COME-UNTO-CHRIST-Forgiveness-MEDITATIONS-ebook/dp/B01N5HJFUW/ref=sr_1_12?ie=UTF8&qid=1505837336&sr=8-12&keywords=Richard+W.+Linford

71. <u>JESUS CHRIST PAPERS</u>. DEATH. DEATH SOLUTION HOW TO AVOID YOUR DEATH?

72. https://www.amazon.com/DEATH-SOLUTION-HOW-AVOID-YOUR-ebook/dp/B01LTGUPZ8/ref=sr_1_49?ie=UTF8&qid=1534869921&sr=8-49&keywords=rICHARD+w+lINFORD

73. <u>JESUS CHRIST PAPERS</u>. HONORING PRESIDENT MARION G. ROMNEY. Noble Apostle of Jesus the Christ the Holy Messiah.

74. https://www.amazon.com/Honoring-President-Marion-G-Romney-ebook/dp/B077GY3ZSX/ref=sr_1_54?ie=UTF8&qid=1534870960&sr=8-54&keywords=rICHARD+w+lINFORD

75. <u>JESUS CHRIST PAPERS</u>: JESUS CHRIST IS THE HOLY MESSIAH: HE SOON WILLL COME TO BEGIN HIS MILLENNIAL REIGN OF PEACE.

76. https://www.amazon.com/JESUS-CHRIST-PAPERS-MESSIAH-MILLENNIAL-ebook/dp/B01EEK4386/ref=sr_1_77?ie=UTF8&qid=1534878985&sr=8-77&keywords=rICHARD+w+lINFORD

77. <u>JESUS CHRIST PAPERS.</u> Meditations on Jesus The Christ and the Book of Mormon, Book of Moroni

78. https://www.amazon.com/Meditations-Jesus-Christ-Mormon-Moroni-ebook/dp/B01MDJT7R7/ref=sr_1_8?ie=UTF8&qid=1502487183&sr=8-8&keywords=Richard+W+Linford

79. <u>JESUS CHRIST PAPERS. ENEMIES.</u> How to get rid of your enemies?

80. https://www.amazon.com/How-get-rid-your-enemies-
ebook/dp/B01KVY0VK8/ref=sr_1_6?ie=UTF8&qid=1505837336&sr=8-
6&keywords=Richard+W.+Linford

81. <u>JESUS CHRIST PAPERS. GRANDPA TO GRANDSON.</u> A letter to my grandson, Jason: You are
a son of our Heavenly Father and Mother. I love you. Your grandpa.

82. <u>JESUS CHRIST PAPERS. GRANDPA. GRANDSON.</u> GOD COULDN'T BE EVERYWHERE SO HE
CREATED GRANDPAS: 692 WAYS TO BE A BETTER GRANDPA TO YOUR GRANDSON.

83. https://www.amazon.com/GOD-COULDNT-EVERYWHERE-CREATED-GRANDPAS-
ebook/dp/B01EKKIAZ2/ref=sr_1_36?ie=UTF8&qid=1534869921&sr=8-
36&keywords=rICHARD+w+lINFORD&dpID=51kbey4orcL&preST=_SY445_QL70_&dpSrc=s
rch

84. <u>JESUS CHRIST PAPERS.</u> HOLINESS! Worship the LORD in the Beauty of Holiness!

85. https://www.amazon.com/HOLINESS-Worship-Beauty-Holiness-Christ-ebook/dp/B06XDHCBS6/ref=sr_1_29?ie=UTF8&qid=1502473575&sr=8-29&keywords=Richard+W+Linford

86. <u>JESUS CHRIST PAPERS.</u> Honoring God the Son whose Second Coming is near: Holy Names, Titles and Concepts that describe Jehovah Jesus Christ The Holy Messiah

87. https://www.amazon.com/Honoring-whose-Second-Coming-near/dp/1521473811/ref=sr_1_30?ie=UTF8&qid=1505838733&sr=8-30&keywords=Richard+W.+Linford

88. <u>JESUS CHRIST PAPERS.</u> Meditations on The Book of [the Prophet] Jacob as found in the [Holy] Book of Mormon including Meditations on The Prophet [Zenos'] Allegory of the Tame and Wild Olive Trees.

89. https://www.amazon.com/Meditations-Book-Mormon-Prophet-Jacob-ebook/dp/B07F98LM3V/ref=sr_1_38?ie=UTF8&qid=1534869921&sr=8-38&keywords=rICHARD+w+lINFORD&dpID=611X8baOG4L&preST=_SY445_QL70_&dpSrc=srch

90. JESUS CHRIST PAPERS. The Holy Ghost Power and Gift.

91. https://www.amazon.com/Holy-Ghost-Power-Gift-Meditations-ebook/dp/B06W2KB7MZ/ref=sr_1_48?ie=UTF8&qid=1534869921&sr=8-48&keywords=rICHARD+w+lINFORD

92. <u>JESUS CHRIST PAPERS</u>. Honoring God the Son whose Second Coming is Near; Holy Names and Concepts that describe Jehovah Jesus Christ The Holy Messiah.

93. <u>https://www.amazon.com/Honoring-whose-Second-Coming-near/dp/1521473811/ref=sr_1_64?ie=UTF8&qid=1534870960&sr=8-64&keywords=rICHARD+w+lINFORD</u>

94. <u>JESUS CHRIST PAPERS.</u> Honoring Moses and Thomas S. Monson, Prophets of God.

95. <u>https://www.amazon.com/Honoring-Moses-Thomas-Monson-Prophets/dp/1521399239/ref=sr_1_23?ie=UTF8&qid=1502473575&sr=8-23&keywords=Richard+W+Linford</u>

96. JESUS CHRIST PAPERS VOLUME 1: THE MANY WITNESSES THAT "HE LIVES!"

97. https://www.amazon.com/Jesus-Christ-Papers-Witnesses-Jehovah/dp/1575740214/ref=sr_1_70?ie=UTF8&qid=1534878985&sr=8-70&keywords=rICHARD+w+lINFORD&dpID=51v8JgbrR9L&preST=_SX218_BO1,204,203,200_QL40_&dpSrc=srch

98. JESUS CHRIST PAPERS. Jesus Christ lives! The many witnesses. Volume 1.

99. https://www.amazon.com/s/ref=sr_pg_6?rh=i%3Aaps%2Ck%3ArICHARD+w+lINFORD&page=6&keywords=rICHARD+w+lINFORD&ie=UTF8&qid=1534878985

100.	JESUS CHRIST PAPERS. Jesus Christ's True Church: 70 characteristics with scriptural references.
101.	https://www.amazon.com/Jesus-Christs-True-Church-characteristics-ebook/dp/B01BO9849E/ref=sr_1_44?ie=UTF8&qid=1534869921&sr=8-44&keywords=rICHARD+w+lINFORD

102.	JESUS CHRIST PAPERS. LIFE. DEATH. he planted Utah strawberries and then he died: richard w Linford
103.	https://www.amazon.com/planted-utah-strawberries-then-died-ebook/dp/B00ZQ1OO64/ref=sr_1_28?ie=UTF8&qid=1502473575&sr=8-28&keywords=Richard+W+Linford

104.	JESUS CHRIST PAPERS. MARRIAGE. Choose Your Love! Love Your Choice! 22 Anti-divorce Principles for Christian Couples.

105.	https://www.amazon.com/Choose-Your-Love-Choice-Anti-divorce-ebook/dp/B011EQ9KSG/ref=sr_1_21?ie=UTF8&qid=1534868802&sr=8-21&keywords=rICHARD+w+lINFORD&dpID=61DnI9110OL&preST=_SY445_QL70_&dpSrc=srch

106.	JESUS CHRIST PAPERS. MEDITATIONS on "THE IMITATION OF CHRIST by Thomas A Kempis" BOOK ONE "Admonitions Profitable for the Spiritual Life": Translated by Rev. William Benham. Meditations by Richard W. Linford. https://www.amazon.com/MEDITATIONS-IMITATION-Admonitions-Profitable-Spiritual-ebook/dp/B01L2SANDW/ref=sr_1_4?ie=UTF8&qid=1502471298&sr=8-4&keywords=Richard+W.+Linford

107.	<u>JESUS CHRIST PAPERS.</u> Meditations on Jesus the Christ and the Book of Mormon, Book of Moroni - Come unto Christ and be perfected in Him. Read the Book of Mormon at <u>**www.lds.org**</u>. Ask God if these things are not true.

108.	https://www.amazon.com/Meditations-Jesus-Christ-Mormon-Moroni-ebook/dp/B01MDJT7R7/ref=sr_1_6?ie=UTF8&qid=1502484088&sr=8-6&keywords=richard+linford

109.	<u>JESUS CHRIST PAPERS. PEACE.</u> PUT DOWN YOUR THOUSAND STONES – Peace between Muslim, Jew and Christian – 304 thoughts - With all thy being, be at peace!

110.	https://www.amazon.com/PUT-DOWN-YOUR-THOUSAND-STONES-ebook/dp/B01DREDVC4/ref=sr_1_12?ie=UTF8&qid=1534865760&sr=8-12&keywords=rICHARD+w+lINFORD

111.	<u>JESUS CHRIST PAPERS. PERSECUTION.</u> HAUN'S MILL TREBLINKA TOO: The Persecution.

112.	<u>https://www.amazon.com/HAUNS-MILL-TREBLINKA-TOO-Persecution-ebook/dp/B0106R3T0Y/ref=sr_1_42?ie=UTF8&qid=1534869921&sr=8-42&keywords=rICHARD+w+lINFORD</u>

113.	<u>JESUS CHRIST PAPERS. PRAYER.</u> PRAY ALWAYS TO OUR FATHER IN HEAVEN IN THE SACRED NAME OF HIS BELOVED SON JESUS CHRIST: The Purifying Power of Humble Prayer.

114.	<u>https://www.amazon.com/ALWAYS-FATHER-HEAVEN-SACRED-BELOVED-ebook/dp/B01GWD5FSU/ref=sr_1_75?ie=UTF8&qid=1534878985&sr=8-75&keywords=rICHARD+w+lINFORD</u>

115. <u>JESUS CHRIST PAPERS. PRIESTHOOD KEYS. APOSTOLIC KEYS.</u> All Apostolic Keys of the Holy Priesthood and Kingdom of God were conferred upon the Prophet Joseph Smith.

116. <u>https://www.amazon.com/APOSTOLIC-KEYS-Apostolic-Priesthood-conferred-ebook/dp/B01BPSQID8/ref=sr_1_35?ie=UTF8&qid=1534869792&sr=8-35&keywords=rICHARD+w+lINFORD</u>

117. <u>JESUS CHRIST PAPERS. REPENT.</u> Repent America or Be Destroyed Like the Jaredites! Repent and Serve The God of This Land who is Jesus Christ!

118. <u>JESUS CHRIST PAPERS</u> – The Father, The Son, The Holy Ghost – Our Divine Origin, Mortality and Destiny.

119. <u>https://www.amazon.com/Jesus-Christ-Papers-Mortality-Destiny-ebook/dp/B01GEYJ47K/ref=sr_1_57?ie=UTF8&qid=1534870960&sr=8-57&keywords=rICHARD+w+lINFORD</u>

120.   <u>JESUS CHRIST PAPERS.</u> THE HOLY GHOST. POWER AND GIFT. MEDITATIONS.

121.   https://www.amazon.com/Holy-Ghost-Power-Gift-Meditations-ebook/dp/B06W2KB7MZ/ref=sr_1_30?ie=UTF8&qid=1502473575&sr=8-30&keywords=Richard+W+Linford

122.   **<u>JESUS CHRIST PAPERS.</u> THE LION OF JUDAH ROARS! REPENT!**

123.   https://www.amazon.com/LION-JUDAH-ROARS-REPENT-Jehovah-ebook/dp/B00ZVB02DS/ref=sr_1_92?ie=UTF8&qid=1534883070&sr=8-92&keywords=rICHARD+w+lINFORD

124.	JESUS CHRIST PAPERS. THE MANY WITNESSES THAT "HE LIVES!"

125.	https://www.amazon.com/Jesus-Christ-Papers-Witnesses-Jehovah/dp/1575740214/ref=sr_1_35?ie=UTF8&qid=1505840223&sr=8-35&keywords=Richard+W.+Linford

126.	JESUS CHRIST PAPERS. THE SECOND COMING OF JESUS CHRIST THE MESSIAH Libretto Sacred Oratorio. The Second Coming as a destruction from the Almighty is near! Repent!

127.	https://www.amazon.com/SECOND-COMING-MESSIAH-Libretto-Oratorio-ebook/dp/B0103H3U0Q/ref=sr_1_91?ie=UTF8&qid=1534883070&sr=8-91&keywords=rICHARD+w+lINFORD

128.	<u>JESUS CHRIST PAPERS. SABBATH BREAKING.</u> Sabbath Breaking and Sports as The Worlds' Religion: Fix it Richard!
129.	<u>https://www.amazon.com/Sabbath-Breaking-Sports-Worlds-Religion-ebook/dp/B010MJFH06/ref=sr_1_31?ie=UTF8&qid=1502473575&sr=8-31&keywords=Richard+W+Linford</u>

130.	<u>JESUS CHRIST PAPERS.</u> Would Jesus Christ Do That? Is the first question!
131.	<u>https://www.amazon.com/Would-Jesus-Christ-first-question/dp/1575740168/ref=sr_1_25?ie=UTF8&qid=1505838470&sr=8-25&keywords=Richard+W.+Linford</u>

132.	<u>MAKE MORE PEPPERONI "MONEY."</u> How to Make More Pepperoni?: How did Steven Jobs; Fed de Luca; Warren Buffett; Bill Gates; Larry Ellison; Carlos Slim; Fred, Charles, David Koch; do it.

133.	<u>MATEO CERVANTES SERIES. NOVEL</u>. Mateo Cervantes - The Old Cowboy Prospector and The Buckskin Rocinante

134.	MELANIA TRUMP. MELANIA TRUMP – HONORING
FLOTUS. https://www.amazon.com/MELANIA-TRUMP-Honoring-FLOTUS-intelligent/dp/1521995273/ref=sr_1_2?ie=UTF8&qid=1502471298&sr=8-2&keywords=Richard+W.+Linford

135.	MARRIAGE. 7 MARRIAGE GIFTS FOR 7 DAYS: To make your good marriage great or your bad marriage better.

136.	https://www.amazon.com/Marriage-Gifts-Days-marriage-better/dp/1575740249/ref=sr_1_69?ie=UTF8&qid=1534878985&sr=8-69&keywords=rICHARD+w+lINFORD&dpID=41pb0KXJj-L&preST=_SX218_BO1,204,203,200_QL40_&dpSrc=srch

137.   <u>MARRIAGE.</u> 199 Ways To Make Your Good Marriage Great or Your Bad marriage Better: Romance and improve your marriage today.

138.   <u>https://www.amazon.com/Ways-Make-Marriage-Great-Better/dp/1575740184/ref=sr_1_14?ie=UTF8&qid=1502487183&sr=8-14&keywords=Richard+W+Linford</u>

139.   <u>https://www.amazon.com/Ways-Make-Marriage-Great-Better/dp/1575740184/ref=sr_1_66?ie=UTF8&qid=1534878879&sr=8-66&keywords=rICHARD+w+lINFORD</u>

140.   <u>MONEY.</u> How to Make More Pepperoni? How did Steven Jobs; Fred de Luca; Warren Buffett; Bill Gates; Larry Ellison; Carlos Slim; Fred, Charles, David Koch; and the Waltons make more pepperoni and how can you?

141.   <u>https://www.amazon.com/How-Make-More-Pepperoni-pepperoni-ebook/dp/B011F4WZP2/ref=sr_1_9?ie=UTF8&qid=1502487183&sr=8-9&keywords=Richard+W+Linford</u>

142.   MUSTANGS. COWBOY POETRY. Mustangs Running With The Judas Horse: How to Write Cowboy Poetry.

143.   https://www.amazon.com/Mustangs-Running-Judas-Horse-Cowboy-ebook/dp/B010OTOLS8/ref=sr_1_88?ie=UTF8&qid=1534883070&sr=8-88&keywords=rICHARD+w+lINFORD

144.   PERFORMANCE AND SUCCESS. Honoring Stephen R Covey October 24, 1932 to July 16, 2012 Life is not accumulation! Think win-win!

145.   https://www.amazon.com/HONORING-STEPHEN-COVEY-October-1932-ebook/dp/B0784CYSJJ/ref=sr_1_59?ie=UTF8&qid=1534870960&sr=8-59&keywords=rICHARD+w+lINFORD

146.   <u>PERFORMANCE AND SUCCESS.</u> Push Your Limits! Honoring General John Francis Kelly! Semper Fidelis! [Always faithful! Always loyal!] The marines have landed at the US White House!

147.   <u>https://www.amazon.com/Limits-Honoring-General-Francis-Fidelis/dp/1522066187/ref=sr_1_1?ie=UTF8&qid=1502471298&sr=8-1&keywords=Richard+W.+Linford</u>

148.   <u>PERFORMANCE AND SUCCESS.</u> PUSH YOUR LIMITS! Honoring Ueli Steck with His two Golden Ice Axes In memoriam. A revolutionary way to live your life by challenging and speed climbing your seemingly impossible physical and spiritual mountains.

149.   <u>https://www.amazon.com/limits-Honoring-Steck-Golden-memoriam-ebook/dp/B0727ZL9QS/ref=sr_1_10?ie=UTF8&qid=1502484088&sr=8-10&keywords=richard+linford</u>

150.	<u>POLITICS</u>. DID THE PATIENT DIE ON THE OPERATING TABLE? OBAMACARE 101 THOUGHTS: Is Obama's "Affordable Health Care" Plan affordable? Is Universal Health Care the answer?

151.	https://www.amazon.com/PATIENT-OPERATING-TABLE-OBAMACARE-THOUGHTS-ebook/dp/B01DOR17HU/ref=sr_1_79?ie=UTF8&qid=1534878985&sr=8-79&keywords=rICHARD+w+lINFORD

152.	<u>POLITICS</u>. DONALD TRUMP: 307 Promises and Positions

153.	https://www.amazon.com/DONALD-TRUMP-307-Promises-Positions-ebook/dp/B01BWDHLVO/ref=sr_1_7?ie=UTF8&qid=1502487183&sr=8-7&keywords=Richard+W+Linford

154.	<u>POLITICS</u>. KILLING BILL O'REILLY. The LEFT tried to KILL BILL'S CAREER! They failed! Bill is back with a VENGEANCE!

155.	https://www.amazon.com/KILLING-BILL-OREILLY-CAREER-VENGEANCE-ebook/dp/B077SH9Z1X/ref=sr_1_3?ie=UTF8&qid=1534865760&sr=8-3&keywords=rICHARD+w+lINFORD

156.	<u>POLITICS</u>. 19 Executive Orders I Recommend President Obama sign Before He Leaves Office.

157.	https://www.amazon.com/Executive-Orders-Recommend-President-Obama-ebook/dp/B010ODV0TM/ref=sr_1_89?ie=UTF8&qid=1534883070&sr=8-89&keywords=rICHARD+w+lINFORD

158.	<u>POLITICS</u>. 50 Reasons to Honor President Barak Obama!: Even if you didn't vote for him!

159.	https://www.amazon.com/Reasons-Honor-President-Barack-Obama-ebook/dp/B010OD6FOC/ref=sr_1_15?ie=UTF8&qid=1534865760&sr=8-15&keywords=rICHARD+w+lINFORD

160.	<u>POLITICS.</u> 50 Reasons to Honor President George W. Bush!: Even if you didn't vote for him!

161.	https://www.amazon.com/Reasons-Honor-President-George-Bush-ebook/dp/B012PG4KSE/ref=sr_1_8?ie=UTF8&qid=1502484088&sr=8-8&keywords=richard+linford

162.	<u>POLITICS</u>. 28 Reasons I WILL NOT VOTE FOR Hillary Clinton and Tim Kaine in November! 30 Reasons I will VOTE FOR PRESIDENT DONALD TRUMP.

163.	https://www.amazon.com/Reasons-Hillary-November-PRESIDENT-President-ebook/dp/B01KWEX9MO/ref=sr_1_39?ie=UTF8&qid=1534869921&sr=8-39&keywords=rICHARD+w+lINFORD

164.	<u>POLITICS</u>. Marty Mouse and The UK Brexit High Anxiety Hotel and Restaurant. A long story. An allegory.

165.	https://www.amazon.com/Marty-Mouse-Brexit-Anxiety-Restaurant/dp/152109649X/ref=sr_1_27?ie=UTF8&qid=1502473575&sr=8-27&keywords=Richard+W+Linford

166. <u>POLITICS.</u> North Korea Solution – THE UNIFIED REPUBLIC OF KOREA! Tear down that DMZ wall Wise Leader Kim Jong-un! President Donald J. Trump.

167. <u>https://www.amazon.com/North-Korea-Solution-President-peacefully/dp/1521131716/ref=sr_1_26?ie=UTF8&qid=1502473575&sr=8-26&keywords=Richard+W+Linford</u>

168. **POLITICS. Repent America or Be Destroyed Like the Jaredites!**

169. <u>https://www.amazon.com/Repent-America-Destroyed-Like-Jaredites-ebook/dp/B013FDG8L8/ref=sr_1_82?ie=UTF8&qid=1534878985&sr=8-82&keywords=rICHARD+w+lINFORD</u>

170.	POLITICS. THE ART OF THE STEAL – THE LITTLE RED POLITICAL BIBLE, ALMANAC, AND CAMPAIGN HANDBOOK. 237 LESSONS FROM THE 2015-2016 TRUMP AND OTHER AMERICAN POLITICAL CAMPAIGNS.

171.	https://www.amazon.com/ART-STEAL-POLITICAL-2015-2016-CAMPAIGNS-ebook/dp/B01E7K829E/ref=sr_1_15?ie=UTF8&qid=1502487183&sr=8-15&keywords=Richard+W+Linford

172.	**POLITICS. TRUMP: NO THIRD TERM IN WHITE HOUSE FOR BILL AND HILLARY CLINTON!: TRUMP Pence LANDSLIDE! Follow blog.**

173.	https://www.amazon.com/TRUMP-HILLARY-CLINTON-LANDSLIDE-richlinfordreport-com-ebook/dp/B01LP5JR2U/ref=sr_1_72?ie=UTF8&qid=1534878985&sr=8-72&keywords=rICHARD+w+lINFORD

174.   <u>PRACTICE. The Power of Best Practice and Best Practices.</u>

175.   https://www.amazon.com/Power-Best-Practice-Practices/dp/1521361398/ref=sr_1_26?ie=UTF8&qid=1534868802&sr=8-26&keywords=rICHARD+w+lINFORD

176.   <u>RAINMAKING.</u> BUSINESS DEVELOPMENT. RAINMAKER, WHO STOPPED THE RAIN DANCE AND TURNED OFF MY RAIN? Rainmaking for lawyers and non-lawyers.

177.   https://www.amazon.com/RAINMAKER-STOPPED-RAIN-DANCE-TURNED-ebook/dp/B00Q7QH9NC/ref=sr_1_11?ie=UTF8&qid=1502487183&sr=8-11&keywords=Richard+W+Linford

178.	SILENCE. In Search of Silence.

179.	https://www.amazon.com/Search-Silence-521-quiet-thoughts-ebook/dp/B01M7UCRX8/ref=sr_1_10?ie=UTF8&qid=1505837336&sr=8-10&keywords=Richard+W.+Linford

180.	SPEED LEARNING. SPEED READING. Speed Learning Checklists: How to speed learn your way to greater expertise and fortune.

181.	https://www.amazon.com/Speed-Learning-Checklists-greater-expertise-ebook/dp/B0106L853G/ref=sr_1_11?ie=UTF8&qid=1505837336&sr=8-11&keywords=Richard+W.+Linford

182.   SURVIVAL CHECKLIST HANDBOOK.

183.   https://www.amazon.com/SURVIVAL-CHECKLIST-HANDBOOK-Principles-Checklists-ebook/dp/B00PXLSD6E/ref=sr_1_15?ie=UTF8&qid=1505837336&sr=8-15&keywords=Richard+W.+Linford

184.   TESTOSTERONE. ABS. ED. LOW TESTOSTERONE, ED, AND 6-8 PACK ABS: 558 thoughts to help you maintain and increase your T, overcome ED, and build 608 Pack Abs.

185.   https://www.amazon.com/LOW-TESTOSTERONE-6-8-PACK-ABS-ebook/dp/B01BCX3Q90/ref=sr_1_16?ie=UTF8&qid=1505837336&sr=8-16&keywords=Richard+W.+Linford

186.	THINK. Think and Grow Smart! Think and Grow Rich! The Story of Ineptitude and the foolish cutting of the Golconda Great Mogul Diamond – The Largest Diamond Found in India Coupled with 50 Tried and True Ancient and Modern Knowledge and Wealth Wisdom Principles

187.	https://www.amazon.com/Think-Grow-Smart-Rich-Principles/dp/1521710155/ref=sr_1_21?ie=UTF8&qid=1502473575&sr=8-21&keywords=Richard+W+Linford

188.	TIME. 730 Ways to Compress and Extend Your Time and Get More Done. For Businesses, Non-profit organizations, Professional firms, Librarians, and Clergy who have SO MUCH TO ACCOMPLISH! SO LITTLE TIME!

189.	https://www.amazon.com/Ways-Compress-Extend-Your-Time-ebook/dp/B012BLRWFG/ref=sr_1_18?ie=UTF8&qid=1534868603&sr=8-18&keywords=rICHARD+w+lINFORD

190.	<u>TIME</u>. Waiting with Brutus Caesar Anthony the 7th and William and Mary Waiting for SAM THE MECHANIC MAN, A long story. An allegory for our auto-driven times. I write. You read. You decide.

191.	https://www.amazon.com/Waiting-Brutus-Anthony-William-MECHANIC/dp/1521158010/ref=sr_1_25?ie=UTF8&qid=1502473575&sr=8-25&keywords=Richard+W+Linford

192.	UNICORN. The White Unicorn Code: Mystery of the Lady with the Unicorn and other Unicorn tapestries

193.	https://www.amazon.com/White-Unicorn-Code-Mystery-tapestries/dp/1452852383/ref=sr_1_13?ie=UTF8&qid=1502487183&sr=8-13&keywords=Richard+W+Linford

194.	<u>WEIGHT REDUCTION.</u> HIGH FRUCTOSE CORN SYRUP AND SUGAR BELLY: 550 thoughts to help you lose your ugly fat and rip your set of six or eight pack abs no matter your age!

195.	https://www.amazon.com/HIGH-FRUCTOSE-SYRUP-SUGAR-BELLY-ebook/dp/B01B554JAK/ref=sr_1_20?ie=UTF8&qid=1534868802&sr=8-20&keywords=rICHARD+w+lINFORD&dpID=617Lfk2i3XL&preST=_SY445_QL70_&dpSrc=srch

196.	<u>WORLD PRISON REFORM SOLUTIONS?</u> 2016 – 2017 INDUSTRIAL RESEARCH REPORT In Search of Prison Reform -- Are our prisons an ethical stain on American society?

197.	https://www.amazon.com/WORLD-PRISON-REFORM-SOLUTIONS-2016-ebook/dp/B01N3LDTJ5/ref=sr_1_7?ie=UTF8&qid=1505837336&sr=8-7&keywords=Richard+W.+Linford

198.	WORLD ANTI-TERRORISM SOLUTIONS IN SEARCH OF POSITIVE WAYS TO ELIMINATE TERRORISM 2016 – 2017 COUNTER TERRORISM RESEARCH REPORT 1st Edition

199.	WORLD WATER SOLUTIONS? 2016 – 2017 INDUSTRIAL RESEARCH REPORT: AIR TO WATER MACHINES. This Industrial Report surveys information available about Air to Water Machines and Air to Water Technology and begins after paragraph 54.

200.	WORLD WATER SOLUTIONS? 2016 – 2017 INDUSTRIAL RESEARCH REPORT: CHEAP? WATER PURIFICATION, SALT WATER DESALINATION, ATMOSPHERIC WATER GENERATION

201.	https://www.amazon.com/WORLD-WATER-SOLUTIONS-2016-PURIFICATION-ebook/dp/B01M12XHTA/ref=sr_1_32?ie=UTF8&qid=1502473575&sr=8-32&keywords=Richard+W+Linford

202.   YOU ARE GREAT. YOU HAVE THE POWER! BECAUSE YOU ARE GREAT! Paint yourself a WHITE, BLACK, GREEN, RED, GOLD SWAN today (My free verse poem)

203.   https://www.amazon.com/YOU-HAVE-POWER-BECAUSE-GREAT-ebook/dp/B011D9024K/ref=sr_1_13?ie=UTF8&qid=1534865760&sr=8-13&keywords=rICHARD+w+lINFORD

204.   A Number of Articles and Papers, one of the most read <u>LDS Church Ensign articles</u> is his <u>20 Ways to Make Your Good Marriage Great, Ensign 1983</u>. He was responsible for writing and producing an earlier version of <u>The LDS Church Welfare Services Handbook</u> and <u>Essentials of Home Production and Storage</u> and similar manuals.

205.   <u>A Number of Talks, Poems, and Critical Reports</u>. [Not found at amazon.com.]

My art – 700+ oil and acrylic paintings - is found at
<u>www.richard-w-linford.pixels.com</u>